Lots More
Tell and Draw Stories

by Margaret Jean Oldfield

BOOKS IN THE TELL AND DRAW SERIES

"Tell and Draw Stories"
"More Tell and Draw Stories"
"Lots More Tell and Draw Stories"

Published by:

CREATIVE STORYTIME PRESS

P.O. Box 572
Minneapolis, Minn. 55440

Printed in the United States of America.

ISBN 0-934876-03-7 Paper Binding

ISBN 0-934876-07-X Library Binding

INTRODUCTION

The teacher or librarian who tells these
stories to children may want to change them
according to his or her needs. The storyteller may want to lengthen or shorten them,
or use simpler or more difficult, picturesque
words according to the age of the children.
The storyteller may draw the picture on the
chalkboard or on a large sheet of paper while
telling the story. Children are delighted
to see a picture develop while listening to
a story.

Children may want to draw the animal after
they have heard the story. A child has a
wonderful imagination and may suggest adding
details, especially about colors and other
things that appeal to their sense of sight,
smell, and touch. I hope these stories will
grow and grow with each telling.

CONTENTS

CONTENTS

AMANDA, THE PANDA

My natural home is in the
high mountains of China,
near a country called Tibet.

I do look like a bear because
of my bulky body and bear-like
head............ but I am
actually a member of the
raccoon family.

I have little black patches
around my eyes.........

My ears are tufts of
black fur........

I am very happy when my
nose............ sniffs
honey, as I think honey
is quite a treat.
I am as fond of honey as
any ordinary bear.

My teeth and mouth.....
are especially adapted
for eating bamboo leaves
and shoots.

Bamboo is a thick, giant
grass that is delicious,
in fact it is my favorite
food except for honey, of
course.
Do you know why bamboo is
called bamboo? When this
thick, giant grass is burned,
it makes a sound that goes
BAM! BOO! BAM! BOO!
And that is how bamboo got
it's name.

My front legs and paws are
entirely black..........
My claws are sharp and
curved. They help me to
climb trees. I can climb
trees as well as any bear.

My back paws and legs are also black........
I am able to bend my toes on my feet backward
and forward. This makes it possible for me to
hold bamboo when I am eating.
AMANDA, THE PANDA spends much of her time munching
on fresh bamboo shoots.

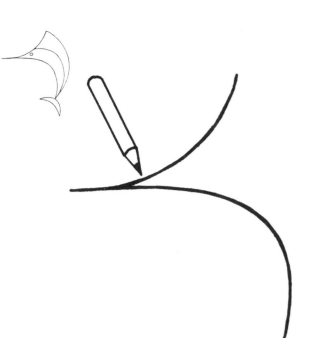

GAIL, THE SAILFISH

Gail, the Sailfish lives in the semi-tropical waters of the Atlantic and Pacific oceans.

Gail's jaw is shaped like a long pointed spear........

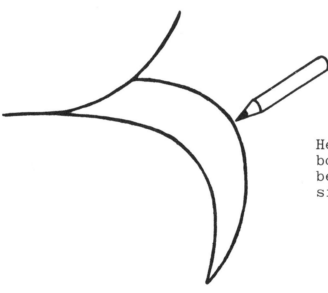

Her torpedo shaped body........ is a beautiful, shimmering silver-blue color.

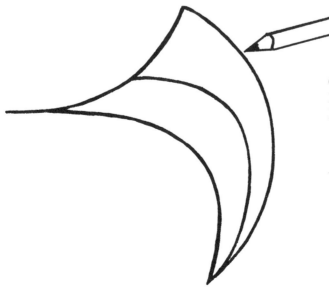

Gail, the Sailfish has a huge fin on her back......... It is so huge that it looks like the sail on a small sail boat. This huge fin, that looks like a sail, is why Gail is called a Sailfish.

Gail is always on the look-out for mackerel, squid and other small fish........
She thinks they make a very delicious meal. Gail weighs about 50 pounds, which is an average weight for a sailfish.

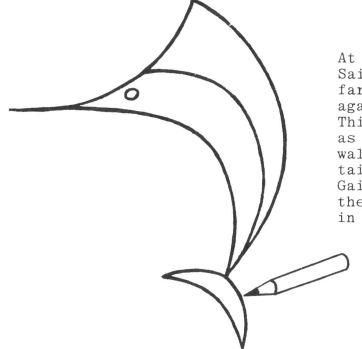

At times Gail, the Sailfish will leap far into the air again and again. This makes her look as though she is walking on her tail......
Gail is also one of the fastest swimmers in the fish world.

Christmas will be coming soon. There is much excitement at
the North Pole where Santa Claus is busy- busy- busy.
I'm sure everyone knows what Santa Claus looks like.

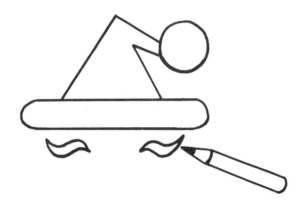

He has a jaunty, little, red hat.
A perky, white pompom hangs right
on the tip just like this........

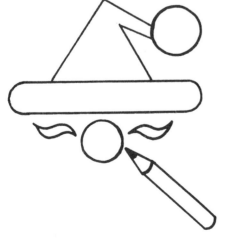

His eyes are crinkly and
sparkling with fun and
laughter...........

His nose is red...... because
it gets awfully cold at the
North Pole where Santa Claus
lives.

A little, white moustache sticks
out below his red nose........

Santa has a very, very large
bushy beard that looks just
like this........

Santa Claus looks quite jolly and happy. Christmas is
the merriest time of year for him because he enjoys giving
toys to children.

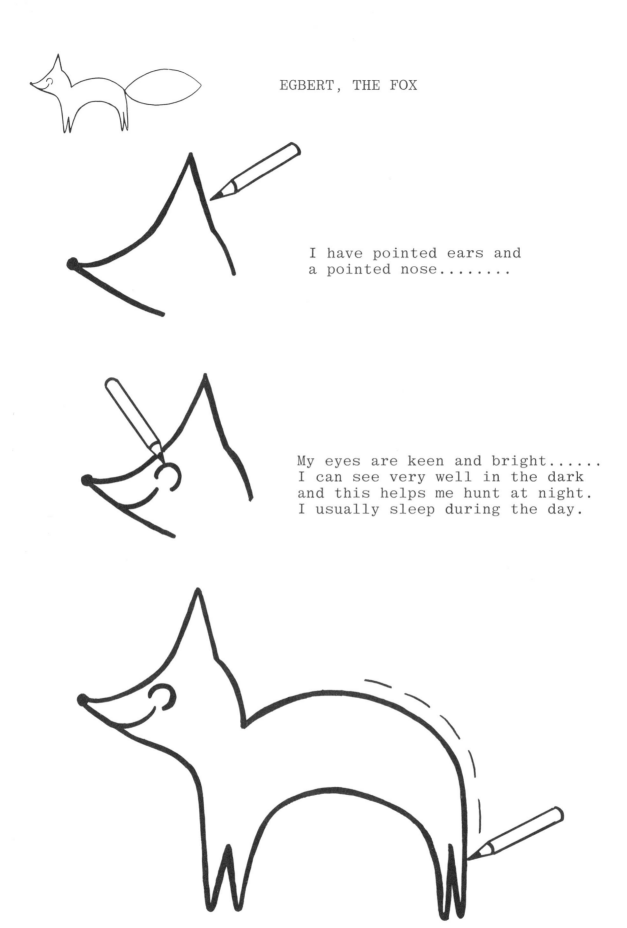

EGBERT, THE FOX

I have pointed ears and
a pointed nose........

My eyes are keen and bright......
I can see very well in the dark
and this helps me hunt at night.
I usually sleep during the day.

I can run very, very fast on my four legs........
Everyone thinks I am quick and speedy.

14

My tail is long and bushy........
When I am sleeping I wrap my tail around me
and it keeps me warm.
I am really quite smart.
Smart as a FOX

I am small and wiggly and I have
lots and lots of soft hair......

I am smiling..... because I know a
secret. Soon I will spin a cocoon
and take a nap. While I am sleeping,
a wonderful thing will happen.
I will turn into a beautiful butterfly.

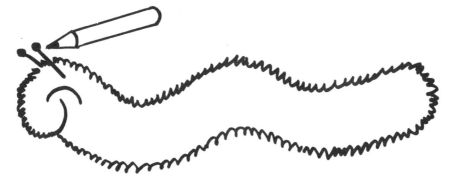

I have two little horns......
They help me feel my way while I am
crawling along.
I am a CATERPILLAR and my world is
very small now.
When I am a butterfly I will be able
to fly over fields, farms and cities.
In fact, I may even fly as far as
South America.

Clementine may also be drawn like this.
If this drawing is used - you would omit
the "lots and lots of soft hair" in the
first part of the story.

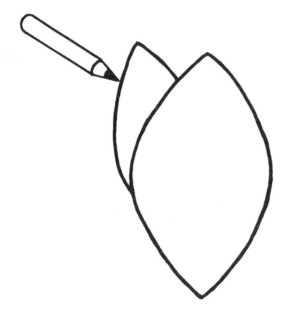

CLEMENTINE, THE BUTTERFLY

Clementine, the Caterpillar
has built a cocoon around
herself.........
The period she is in the
cocoon is called the Pupa
Stage of her life.

When Clementine emerges
from her cocoon she
stretches her wings......

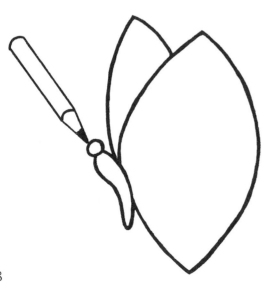

Remember how Clementine
looked as a caterpillar?
Now she looks completely
different. Besides having
new wings, she has a long,
slender body with a small
head..........

18

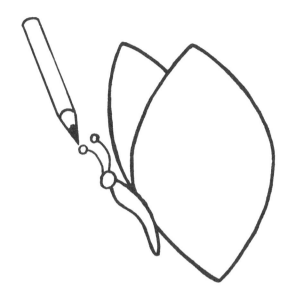

Butterflies have antennae
or feelers.........
Butterfly antennae have
little knobs on the end.

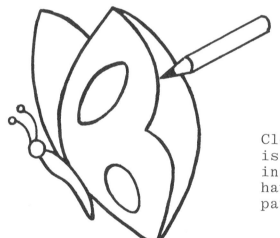

Clementine, the Butterfly
is an extremely beautiful
insect. Her large wings
have bright, brilliant
patterns of color.......

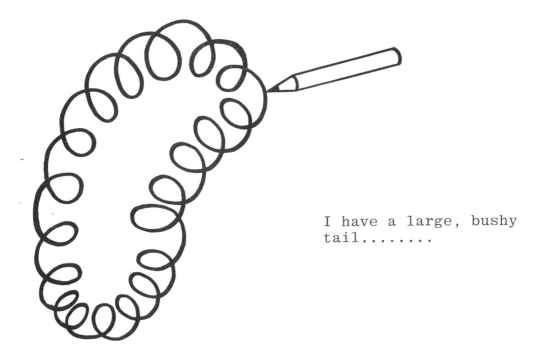

I have a large, bushy
tail........

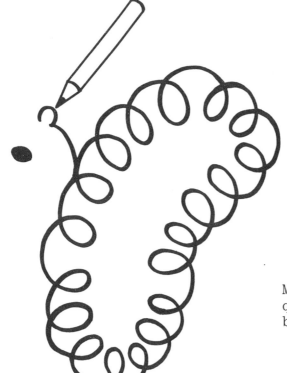

My ears and eyes are
quite small........
but I am very alert.

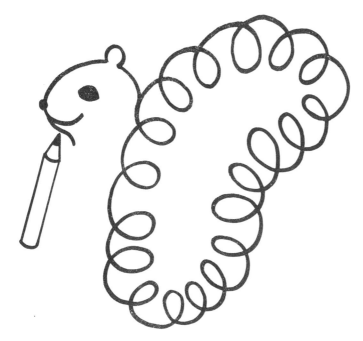

My nose....... helps me find nuts and
berries or even some sunflower seeds.
I carry some of my food in my cheeks
until I can bury it or put it in a hole
in the tree.

My little paws have
little claws.....
They help me to climb
up to the very top of
the tallest tree. They
also help me dig so I
can bury my nuts in
the ground.
Sometimes I forget where I bury a nut
and it grows into a tall tree.
I am a very busy SQUIRREL during the
Summer and Fall, because I am storing
away food. My store of nuts, berries,
and seeds will feed me all Winter.

21

HERBERT, THE HEDGEHOG

I love to eat slugs and worms. I push
back the earth with my sharp little
nose........ to find them.

I also love to eat insects.
My eyes...... are very good at
finding grasshoppers and crickets.

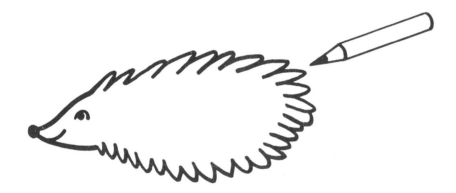

Little quills stick out all over me......
When I am afraid I roll myself into a
prickly little ball. I look just like a
pin cushion. The porcupine is a very
close relative of mine.

22

My legs are quite short.....
because I am quite small.
I am only about 10 inches long.
Our flowers, vegetables and
trees would be destroyed by
harmful bugs without insect
eaters like the HEDGEHOGS.

FAT CAT AND SKINNY WINNIE

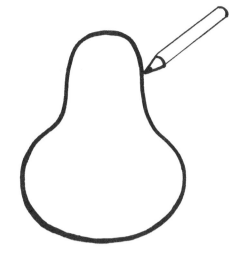

Fat Cat's real name is Petunia but
everyone calls her 'Fat Cat' for
obvious reasons. Skinny Winnie's
real name is Winifred. Fat Cat
and Skinny Winnie are sisters.
They take cat naps in a beautiful
big basket.

This is their basket.........

Fat Cat and Skinny Winnie are so very
proud of their beautiful basket.
They hide all their pussy cat treasures
and toys in their basket with them,
especially their favorite catnip mouses.
This mouse's name is Squeaky and it
belongs to Fat Cat.............
This mouse's name is Ernestine and it
belongs to Skinny Winnie.........

There were two fluffy balls with
jingle bells on them right here......
These were very important toys to
Fat Cat and Skinny Winnie.

And here is a yarn ball with two
strings hanging from it......
Fat Cat and Skinny Winnie are
quite crowded for space when
they have all their toys in
the basket.

At the other end of their basket, they
kept a long piece of string.......,
which they dearly loved to chase.

Skinny Winnie did most
of the chasing.
Fat Cat just liked to sit.

Fat Cat enjoyed sitting in her
basket with her paws tucked under
her like this..........
She would survey the world with
pussy cat contentment.

Fat Cat thought she had a pretty good life.
She had a good home, good food, a good bed,
and a very nice sister.
And she had some very fine whiskers that looked
like this.......

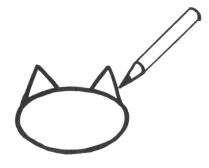

Fat Cat was curled up in a furry
ball like this.........
She was taking a cat nap.
She took many cat naps during
the day.

Suddenly Fat Cat's ears stood
up just like this.......
She had heard the refrigerator
door open. The refrigerator
door opening was one of Fat Cat's
favorite sounds. She knew that
meant food.

Fat Cat took off for the kitchen
just like this.........
Fat Cat ran as fast as a fat cat
could. But when she arrived in
the kitchen, no one was at the
refrigerator.

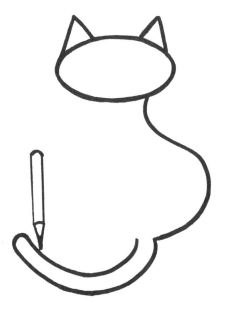

Fat Cat searched all over the
kitchen just like this.......
But she couldn't find even a
small tidbit of food. "Meow",
said Fat Cat, which meant, "I
haven't had a thing to eat for
at least an hour."

Fat Cat decided to look for
Skinny Winnie and discuss the
food situation with her.

Fat Cat jumped up on the shelf
by the window like this......
This shelf was one of Fat Cat
and Skinny Winnie's favorite
places because there was a
splendid view of the birds at
the bird feeder.
Bird watching was Fat Cat's
second favorite hobby.
Of course, Eating was her first
and favorite hobby.

Fat Cat stared bright-eyed at
the bird feeder. There were
three birds feeding on one
side like this........
One bird was a brilliant red
cardinal, the second bird was
a little goldfinch, and the
third bird was a black-capped
chickadee.

Three colorful birds were also
perched on the other side of
the bird feeder like this.....
One bird was a bright blue
bluejay, the second bird was
a little brown sparrow, and
the third bird was a red-headed
woodpecker.
The birds were very glad that
Fat Cat was on the other side
of the window. Fat Cat could
look all she wanted but she
couldn't touch.   "Meow", said
Fat Cat, which meant, "I wish
I could go out and play with them."

One afternoon Fat Cat was busy prowling
and snooping around the kitchen.
She hoped someone had left some milk
or some fish or just anything she could
gobble down.

Fat Cat thought there might be some
goodies on the kitchen counter so she
hopped up like this........

She snooped and sniffed all over the
counter just like this..........
But there was not one tiny morsel
that a cat could eat.

Fat Cat came to a cupboard. She gave
the door a cautious nudge with her
paw like this..........
But the door would not budge, no
matter how hard she nudged.

Fat Cat went on to another cupboard.
The door was open just a crack so she
took her paw and pulled very hard.
The door opened like this........
and Fat Cat strolled in.
The door slammed shut after her.

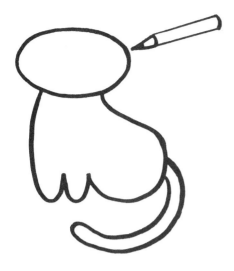

Fat Cat snooped around the cupboard
like this...........
It was filled with all sorts of
goodies that appeal to cats.

A can of savory salmon was sitting in
the middle of the cupboard shelf.....
and two cans of tasty tuna sat right
next to the salmon...........
Fat Cat really wished she had a can
opener but then she would not know
how to use a can opener if she had one.
Have you ever heard of a cat that
could use a can opener?

Fat Cat snooped in another corner and
discovered two cans of cat food for
'finicky' eaters right here......
"Oh, Yum-Yum", said Fat Cat to herself.

Two Boxes of dry, crunchy cat food stood
right over here..........
But Fat Cat could not open either box.

Fat Cat just loved to eat. But
she could not taste any of the
delicious cat food because she
could not open the cans and boxes.
Fat Cat was really quite disgusted
with the situation. She scratched
on the door of the cupboard very
loudly just like this.........
But no one came to let her out
of the cupboard. She scratched
again much louder like this.....

Finally Susan heard her and opened the cupboard door.
Susan was the little girl who lived with Fat Cat and
Skinny Winnie. She was very glad to see Fat Cat as
she had been searching all over the house and calling
for her. Susan gave Fat Cat a tasty tidbit of food.
Fat Cat said "Meow" which means "Thank you.
And she smiled a pussy cat smile about her
adventure in the cupboard.

Skinny Winnie was Fat Cat's sister.
Her real name was Winifred but
everyone called her Skinny Winnie.
She was as skinny as Fat Cat was fat.

Skinny Winnie was sitting on the table
by the window right here.........
She was watching the birds at the bird
feeder. Skinny Winnie thought bird
watching was a lot of fun and just
about the most interesting thing a
cat could do.

Two blue jays sat chattering to each
other right here.........

And over here sat a beautiful, bright
red cardinal.........

Two perky little chickadees perched
right here........

Six fat sparrows fluttered around
the bird feeder like this........

Two squirrels chattered and scurried after the seed that fell on the ground.......

Skinny Winnie perked up her ears. She heard some twittering and tweeting. It was coming from the fireplace. Skinny Winnie ran very fast to the fire-place just like this......

Skinny Winnie was quite surprised to hear that the twittering and tweeting was coming from far up the chimney. She was very curious and she started creeping up the chimney like this...

Because it was cold, a large group of birds were sitting on the chimney enjoying the warmth that came up from the house. They were chirping and cheeping because they were happy and warm.

They didn't know that Skinny Winnie was creeping very slowly up the chimney. She was creeping very slowly because cats aren't used to climbing on bricks. Skinny Winnie slipped on the bricks and down, down she fell just like this.......

"Meow", said Skinny Winnie.
That meant, "I'm all covered with ashes and soot
and all I wanted to do was play with those birds."
She jumped out of the fireplace just like this....
and ran to her secret hiding place in the closet.
Skinny Winnie wanted some privacy while she cleaned
herself with her tongue. She washed her paws and
her tail and her back and her tummy and her face.

Suddenly the closet door opened
slowly just like this........
Skinny Winnie was frightened and
she arched her back.
But can you guess who it was?
It was Fat Cat.
Fat Cat was very good at opening
closet doors especially when she
was looking for Skinny Winnie.

One day Fat Cat and her sister, Skinny Winnie were all alone in their house. They yawned and looked at each other and wondered what they should do. Fat Cat sat here...... and Skinny Winnie sat here......

Fat Cat was thinking delicious thoughts about her favorite subject which was food. "Meow", said Fat Cat to Skinny Winnie.
That meant, "Let's eat"
Fat Cat and Skinny Winnie had a very large food dish right here.........

One little cat yum-yum lay in the dish right here.........
A yum-yum is just like candy for cats.

There were two slurps of milk right here.......

And two bites of salmon right here..........

There were three pieces of fresh,
fragrant fish in the dish on
this side.......
This fish was for Fat Cat.

And three pieces of delectable,
delicious fish for Skinny Winnie
on this side of the dish.......

Skinny Winnie purred and daintily
licked herself. She was quite
satisfied with her meal.
But Fat Cat was not satisfied.
She thought she deserved more.

Fat Cat explored the
kitchen just like
this.......
She was looking for
more delicious tidbits
of food.

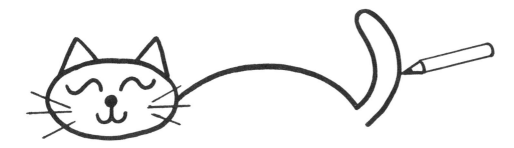

Fat Cat took a running leap and landed up on the
kitchen counter. She was just a little overweight
so she had to jump extra hard. Fat Cat really
needed to go on a diet. She searched the counter
thoroughly like this.........
But she could not find any delicious tidbits.

Fat Cat crept up
on the refrigerator
right here.....
"Meow", said Fat
Cat, which meant.
"Please Open Up"
but the door did
not open.

Fat Cat found the
cupboard where the
cat food was kept
right here.....
She nudged the
door hopefully
with her paw but
no luck.

Fat Cat was
thoroughly
disgusted.
It was awfully
hard for a
pussy cat to
get into
refrigerators
and cupboards.
She lay down
beside her
food dish
right here....
and dreamed
delicious dreams
of fish and milk
and cat yum-yums.

36

One clear, warm night in June, Fat Cat looked up at the
yellow moon. "I think I'd like to go there," thought
Fat Cat. "It might be made of tuna fish".

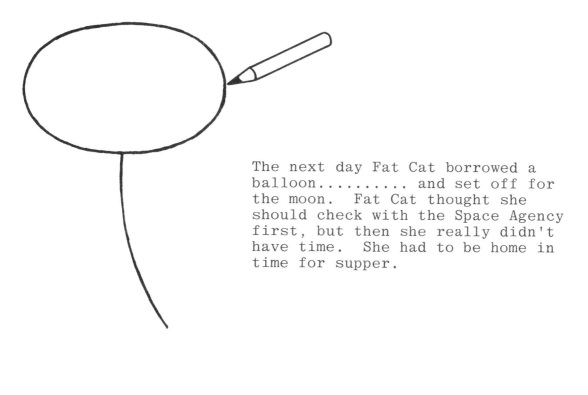

The next day Fat Cat borrowed a
balloon......... and set off for
the moon. Fat Cat thought she
should check with the Space Agency
first, but then she really didn't
have time. She had to be home in
time for supper.

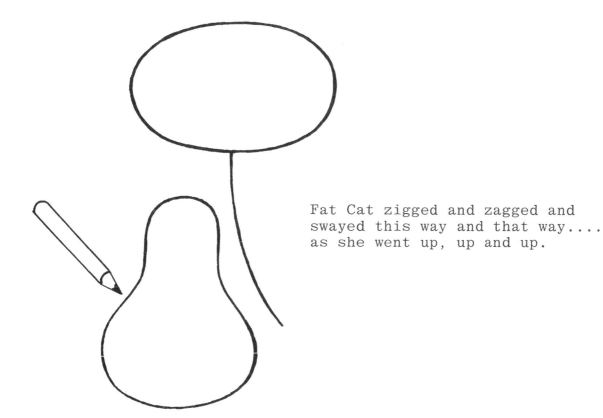

Fat Cat zigged and zagged and
swayed this way and that way....
as she went up, up and up.

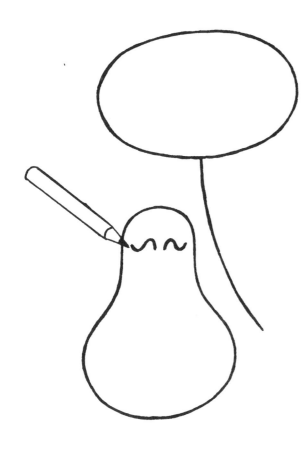

Fat Cat met two birds.......
who were quite surprised to
see a cat flying.
"I'm going to the moon with
my balloon", said Fat Cat
to the birds.

Fat Cat smiled like this.....
because she thought she was
quite a smart cat to be flying.

Fat Cat's ears twitched.......
as she soared higher and higher.
"I hope I reach the moon with my
balloon soon", thought Fat Cat
"because I am getting hungry.

Suddenly Fat Cat started to go
down, down and down..........
Maybe Fat Cat was landing on
the moon or maybe there was
a leak in the balloon.

Fat Cat hung on tight to her
balloon...........
She thought she just might be
landing on the moon.

Fat Cat's whiskers twitched
in anticipation.........
as she thought of eating all
the tuna fish on the moon.

But do you know where she landed?
Fat Cat landed right smack on top
of her own family's garage.
Fat Cat's family had to get a
ladder and climb up on the garage
to rescue Fat Cat. Fat Cat was
afraid to come down by herself.
Luckily Fat Cat did get home in
time for supper.
"I'll try to go to the moon again
next week", thought Fat Cat, and
see if it is made of tuna fish".

Conservation Stories

Stories about water animals
endangered by
man's disregard for nature.
These stories are designed
to stimulate classroom
discussion and develop
environmental concern.

Our streams, ponds, lakes, rivers and oceans have provided a home for living creatures for a very, very long time. Now some of these creatures are in trouble because man is destroying their homes.

One of these creatures is called the
PUPFISH

The pupfish lives in small pools and streams in the Death Valley Desert of California.........

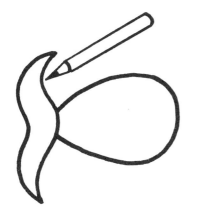

A pupfish is quite frisky and may even wag his tail like a puppy..... That is why he is called a pupfish.

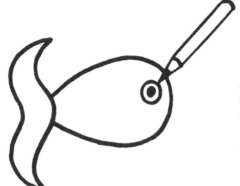

The eye of the pupfish is
very small...........
because this little fish
is extremely tiny. In fact,
he isn't much longer than
your finger.

The pupfish is a happy and very adaptable
resident of Death Valley. He has lived
there since the Ice Age. He has survived
all of the changes nature has made, BUT
he can not survive the changes man is making.

The pupfish will become extinct unless
man stops draining water from pools and
streams in which the pupfish lives.

The ALLIGATOR is another water animal who loses his home when water is removed from swamps and marshes.

The alligator has a large, powerful tail.......

He uses his large, powerful tail to dig water holes when the swamps are very dry. These water holes help other swamp creatures who need water in order to live. The alligator is necessary for the survival of swamp water animals such as frogs, fish and snails.

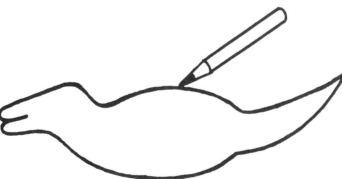

Unfortunately, alligators have valuable hides.........
Men kill the alligator to sell his hide to companies that make shoes, handbags, billfolds, belts and other articles. Laws protect the alligator but this does not prevent the illegal killing of alligators by poachers.

Alligators are satisfied, peaceful residents of
Everglades National Park in Florida........
They are also found throughout the state of Florida
and in Louisiana, Alabama, Mississippi, Georgia,
North Carolina, South Carolina, Texas and Arkansas.

The alligator does not move fast on land because he
has little, short legs...........
He is much more at home in the water, where his large
tail swishes back and forth providing power and speed.

But the alligator is not speedy enough to escape the
poacher, the land developer, the water polluter and
the person who buys articles made from alligator hide.
If we do not have more consideration for the alligator
and the areas where he lives and where he raises his
young - THE ALLIGATOR MAY BECOME EXTINCT.

The pupfish only lives in California, and the alligator only lives in the southeastern part of the United States.

But now we will look at a friendly, feathered water animal who lives in every part of our country.

Ducks and other water birds need WATER....... in order to live. The shores of lakes, ponds and rivers are safe places to build nests, to lay eggs and to raise young ducklings. They also need water that is free from pollution by insecticides and other chemicals.

A duck will often build her nest on the shore of a pond or marsh.......
Mrs. Duck likes the protection of tall grass in marshy areas. Ducklings swim shortly after they hatch. In the water ducklings are safe from fox and other ground animals. If water is drained from swamps and sloughs, ducks will not have a place to build their nests and a place to raise their young.

A duck's bill is designed
just right for eating water
weeds and algae from ponds
and marshes..........
They also eat insects, snails
and some very small water
animals.

Ducks are always on the
lookout for a corn or grain
field........
Happiness to a duck, is
having corn to eat.
So, if you want to make
friends with a duck, be
sure and give him some
delicious corn.

Wouldn't it be sad if we should never be able to see another
pupfish, or alligator or duck again. This could happen if
man does not stop destroying streams, ponds and swamp areas
by drainage or by filling them to make more land. Man must
also make every effort to avoid polluting our water areas
with chemicals and insecticides. Clean water is necessary
for the survival of all animals and man too.

The next story is about Suzanne, The Brown Pelican. Suzanne's
very existence is being threatened by poisonous pesticides.

SUZANNE THE PELICAN

S is for Suzanne.......
Suzanne is a brown pelican.

A pelican has a long,
long bill......

Suzanne has a very large pouch
which hangs from her lower bill....
Pelicans love to eat fish and
they can store many, many fish
in their pouch.

Suzanne has very keen eyesight.....
She can spot a fish in the water
while she is flying.

When Suzanne spots a fish,
she dives into the water
like this......
"Swoosh and Swish, I caught
a fish", says Suzanne.

After Suzanne has had her
dinner of fish, she glides
over the water like this....
Perhaps she is flying back
to shore and her nest.

Suzanne's feet are webbed,
just like a duck's feet....
In fact she waddles when she
walks, just like a duck.

Suzanne and her relatives live
along our coast line, because
they like salt water. Man's
pollution of our coastal waters
by D.D.T. provides fish with
large amounts of this poisonous
pesticide. When Suzanne eats a
fish, she also eats the D.D.T.
which is in the fish. Then when Suzanne lays her eggs, the
shells are very thin because of the effects of the D.D.T.
In fact the shell is so week that it breaks within a few
days. The result is that very few baby brown pelicans have
been hatched. If pelicans are to be saved from extinction,
man must not use D.D.T. and other poisonous chemicals.

Library Cataloging Data:

Oldfield, Margaret Jean. Lots More Tell and Draw Stories

Summary: Eighteen short stories for children from pre-school through the lower elementary grades with chalktalk illustrations.

1. Storytelling. 2. Chalktalk. 3. Wildlife-Conservation-Fiction. I. Title.